2

ANDREW WATERHOUSE

2nd

THE SECOND COLLECTION

The Rialto

ACKNOWLEDGEMENTS

Are due to the editors of the following, and other, magazines who first published some of these poems, *Other Poetry, Oxford Poetry, Smiths Knoll, The North, The Rialto, TLS*. Also to MidNag, who first published, as *Good News from a Small Island*, many of the Lindisfarne poems.

Cover Image: illustration for "Speaking About My Cracked Sump"
© Ian Patience

Photographs: Martin Waterhouse ©

ISBN 0-9527444-4-9

The publisher acknowledges financial assistance from East England Arts and the Arts Council of England

First published in 2002 by *The Rialto*
PO Box 309 Aylsham Norwich
England NR11 6LN

The Rialto is a Registered Charity No. 297553
Typeset in Perpetua 10 on 12.5pt
Design by Starfish, Norwich
Printed by Printing Services (Norwich) Limited

IN MEMORIAM

Andrew Waterhouse 1958 - 2001

CONTENTS

FOREWORD

This is the text that I received of the poems that Andrew Waterhouse had been working on before his death. He had called these 'The Second Collection'; this may have been a working title but it seems appropriate to keep it. There are repetitions - eg the two versions of the bathroom poem - which I have kept in the text, preferring to leave the work as it stands and to wonder what was intended. The piece that Andrew wrote for *The Rialto* about himself and his working methods is included because it shows the poet's great enjoyment of his creativity.

Michael Mackmin

A COLLOQUY

Pupils: Good teacher, why have you brought us to our church ?
Teacher: To continue your studies. Do you wish to learn or to be
beaten ?
Pupils: To learn.
Teacher: Then come closer my children. What do you see ?
Pupils: An oaken coffin, sir.
Teacher: And what of the carving here upon its surface ?
Pupils: We see the Christ.
Teacher: It is good to see the Christ. And in the four corners ?
Pupils: A man incarnate, the eagle who flew again, a calf without
pride, the lion that felt our pains.
Teacher: And here ?
Pupils: Archangels. Michael and Gabriel.
Teacher: And here ?
Pupils: The good Virgin and Child.
Teacher: And how many apostles ?
Pupils: Twelve, sir.
Teacher: And who carries the keys ?
Pupils: St. Peter, sir.
Teacher: What is in this coffin ?
Pupils: A coffin.
Teacher: And within that ?
Pupils: A coffin.
Teacher: And within that ?
Pupils: Our saint.
Teacher: And what holy goods of the saint ?
Pupils: A small altar upon his breast, a jewelled cross, an ivory comb,
a stole, a maniple, scissors, a chalice, a paten, the head of a king, a
book.
Teacher: Tell me more of the book.
Pupils: It is jewelled and speaks the good news.
Teacher: You are good and learned children. The bell is sounding.
Our brothers come. Sing well and pray for our many sins.
Pupils: We will pray for all our sins.

*A "colloquy" was a method used to teach Latin in monastery schools. It involved translating dialogues between teacher and pupils into Old English from Latin and vice versa. Here I am imagining that the monastery teacher on Lindisfarne takes his class to see the coffin of St Cuthbert in the island church and that they construct a colloquy from the conversations.

MODERN GRAMMAR: USE OF THE PERSONAL PRONOUN (NOMINATIVE)

I am a good person,
as are you.

She has just arrived here,
cannot speak English
and is probably a whore.

He looks at children.

It is obvious:
we must stick together.

They need to be dealt with.

LOOKING FOR CUTHBERT'S BEADS

on the northern shore, among the lines
of seaweeds, broken shells, stones, bleached fronds.
They are hard to find, not beautiful;
just rough leaden discs, like Saxon coins,
poorly minted; but older by far,
these broken stems of Crinoidea,
Stone Lily, Feather-Star that once fed
here, but between other continents,
five arms taking in all that passed by.
The islanders used to collect them,
threaded rosaries in hard winters.
Now, it is quiet. Gulls try to laugh
without smiling, waves reach for the land
and I pick this single bead for you,
and smile, turn it over in my hands,
remembering all the devotions.

IS GOD THE TABLE ?

I am looking at my map
on the table in my house.
My house is a black square,
so I must be inside the map.
I fold the map and swallow.
Where am I ? On the table ?
Something carnivorous crawls across the table.
It eats my map inside me.
The carnivorous something
is captured and burnt
by an indigenous people.
My mother is an indigenous
person. She breathes
in the smoke. She grows
more cells. Eventually,
here I am again. Hello.
But where is the table ?
Is God the table ?
Please let God be the table.

IN YOUR BATHROOM

The ceiling is blue and the walls are yellow;
hanging, is a shoal of red and green fish,
turning so slowly, turning so slowly;
among your soaps and creams rest oyster shells,
also limpets and a line of seahorses
ride up towards the true mirror as we float
together in your large bath, steam rising
around us and I lean back against your breasts,
sink between your legs and smiling
you pour water over my face, my hair,
again and again as if I had just emerged,
needing to be woken up and well cleansed
before you could help me onto dry land.

"IN" : THE DIGEST

It being suggested that I get out
of myself, I set off in fine weather
towards the sun and beyond. Full of red, she walked
more quickly. I say: "We'll all be dead
soon" and she laughs
in the forest behind the supermarket.

through crisp grasses where snakes coil and recoil.

There were no tree songs. Many hours pass.
This is a quiet forest

HAIRSTYLES OF THE EVANGELISTS

Matthew is an old hippy,
greying, with a fine pigtail and centrally
parted. He may be the wisest. Mark has gone
a perm too far, like Kevin Keegan
circa 1979, but looks to have two good feet.
Sad Luke's mullet
is a bastard child of the '80's.
Best forgotten.
                     And John stares
out at my back and sides.
He is Marc Bolan
just before he rode away on that white swan.
Give me some Good Words, John.
Just a few Good Words, John.

GOOD NEWS FROM LINDISFARNE

Chord Intro

V1
I signed off the dole,
Sat lotus on the floor,
Became a crooked cabinet maker,
For Lady Eleanor.

Ch
And she met me on the corner,
And the fog had lifted,
Yeah, she met me on the corner,
And all the fog had lifted (yeah).

V2
Everyone did their thing,
Everyone wet the wall,
For that belly dancing beauty,
For Lady Eleanor.

Ch
And she met me on the corner,
And the fog had lifted,
Yeah she met me on the corner,
And all the fog had lifted (yeah).

Mandolin Solo
(quite tricky)

V3
But when the lights come on again,
I promise I'll be there,
Without my rags and my reminders,
Of Lady Eleanor.

Ch
And she met me on the corner,
And the fog had lifted,
Yeah she met me on the corner,
And all the fog had lifted (yeah)

V4
I've stolen some new dreams
For you and me to share
And we'll run for home together
Without Lady Eleanor.

Ch
And she met me on the corner,
And the fog had lifted,
Yeah she met me on the corner,
And all the fog had lifted (yeah)

Yeah
Yeah
Yeah
Yeah
Yeah
Yeah
Yeah
Yeah
Yeah
Yeah
Yeah
Yeah
Yeah
Yeah
(fade out)

*You may recognise some lines from a few songs in this poem.

GOOD NEWS FROM A SMALL ISLAND (A SELECTION FROM A SEQUENCE OF POEMS RELATED TO LINDISFARNE GOSPELS)

Making the Book

1. Eadfrith in the Scriptorium

old and coming to the end, in the seventh year,
of his Great Labour for God and St Cuthbert;
fingers the skins he has smoothed and gathered,
the pages ruled with stylus and that good knife;
the feathers pulled from a goose wing,
cured in boiling sand, slit to the strongest point;
dipped in ink of lamp black and soot;

and now Good Eadfrith mouths all
he has written in sturdy half-uncials as a soldier
of Christ, each word another wound
on Satan's skin, every letter a preaching
with the hand, a glimpse of the Godhead

and now Good Eadfrith sees his illuminations
before him: the first words, evangelists, crossed pages
of pelta and fret and unsmiling he leaves one wing
without feathers, that interlace unreddened,
those few letters empty; in order to remain imperfect,
in order once more to please his God.

2. The Binding of Aethalwald

He squares up the pages, the thirty three gatherings,
trapped between oak boards; he rubs beeswax on the threads
to ease each sewing, glues the spine, hammers it curved;
then lays out the almost book on crimson goatskin,
well pared and pasted, folds the leather inwards and inwards,
smooths it with his hand, rests his fingers on the words;
his opus manuum, his binding.

3. Billfrith the Jeweller

who has stood outstretched with the silence
of waves for some time; now bends,
lifts from the pile two garnets,
red and hard, holds them over the Book's
freshly grown skin, whispers
a question and waits for instructions
and waits as the moon crosses
the glassless window, as the bells
sound beyond the narrows,
as the wind scatters straws
from the thatch and again waits
for the tide that rises then falls
as this late frost gathers
to hold and kiss,
to whiten and kiss
his dirty hands.

4. Aldred the Glossator

wrote between the lines his thick mouthed translation
in insular miniscule, cursive and quick
as if it were business or the Law; thinking himself unworthy
and most miserable, seeking the help
of God and his saint for a steady hand and hard eye
as the snow fell and the snow fell
in Chester-le-Street that winter and the light moved on elsewhere.

* *Eadfrith was the scribe and illustrator of The Lindisfarne Gospels,
Aethalwald bound the book and Billfrith the Anchorite decorated its cover
with gold and jewels. Two hundred and fifty years later, Aldred, a priest of
Chester-le-Street, wrote an Old English translation between the lines of the
original Latin text.*

THIS ONE MIXES UP THE END OF A RELATIONSHIP AND CHOPPING FIREWOOD

My Firewood Therapy

axe fall
catching light
what was one
is now two
blade halving
the bark
the bast
the xylem
cutting heartwood years
every slice thinning
as memory should
to a splinter
just beyond sight
to the final cell
my hand unsteady
wall now breached

organelles
spill out are lost
on the woodshed floor
no way back
but to cut
into the matrix
the cavities and membranes
the protein webs

breaking the long chains
towards a single molecule
to the lone atom
spinning in the dark

surrounded by uncertainty
still at the core

two particles to be split

DIAPAUSING

That need to crawl under a stone
or deep among dead leaves;
to let the blood snail and thicken,
as a second skin grows
over these spineless dreams.

COMING DOWN FROM HART CRAG

This could be
a thin stream
or the right path.
We might be
in low cloud
or under the sea.
I may be crying
or rain streaked.
I could love you
or could not,
but need to know
before we reach the flat ground.

CHAIR

Facing the sea, washed out of some office
or waiting room long ago; now reduced, essential,
tubular; in profile, a letter, but not of our language,
offering no comfort or support; the metal reddened,
bruised, proud of its mild diseases, of its survival,
as the wind turns again, warm air from the south
fluting a note, that shifts a semi-tone and back;
that chair on the longshore, singing.

BUTTERFLY ON STAINED GLASS

Church of St. Mary the Virgin, Holy Island

is undecided, at the dead saint's feet;
having rested well since October;
but now, needing more light and heat,
stumbles from brown sandals, to grey cowl,
to pink hand, then finds that clear glass
with blue sky behind, settles, and the sun
illuminates her outstretched wings:
each uncounted scale laid out between veins,
the red-orange sheen, black and yellow patches,
blue lunules on the margins

                                 and I reach up,
cup her in my hands, walk through old incense
from transept to porch, to the open door,
release her into this day, her unsteady wings
catching the light again over celandines
and gravestones and on towards the sea.

ENJOYING AN EXHIBITION AT THE BRITISH LIBRARY

Doing avoidance and fouled temper,
I move from you to a Hard Day's Night
(4/10, see me wrote Lennon
at the bottom) and then to Scott's concern
about his feet, five early Shakespeare's,
one declaration of war, the Koran,
a map of the world, various Bibles;
and so on until here is the Book,
still open after thirteen hundred years,
resting in its own dark optima
(lux around 40, also the heat
and humidity of a June morning)
and yes here is the Book open today
on St John's and I lean into it,
open mouthed, my breath on the glass
slowing, as I count twelve marginal dogs;
trace unbreakable frets and keyworks;
and I'm seeing and not seeing
and I'm not seeing and seeing,
that central crucifix packed with interlace;
that bird maze in the background,
all crazy eyed, hooked on their neighbours,
mouths clasping necks, legs, other mouths;
woven like the worst of all families
as if it were a cartoon orgy
or advanced cannibalism.
"A mandala," you say before leaving.
"Is that the Supreme Being
or just your Higher Self,
you're staring at ?"

BILLFRITH THE ANCHORITE

who has stood outstretched with the silence
of waves for some time; now bends,
lifts from the pile two garnets,
red and set, holds them over the Book's
freshly grown skin, whispers
a question and waits for instructions
and waits as the moon crosses
the glassless window, as the bells
sound beyond the narrows,
as the wind scatters straws
from the thatch and again waits
for the tide that rises then falls
as this late frost gathers
to hold and kiss,
to whiten and kiss
his dirty hands.

BATH-TIME

For Hala

The ceiling is blue and the walls are yellow;
hanging, is a shoal of red and green fish,
turning so slowly, turning so slowly;
among your soaps and creams rest oyster shells,
also limpets and a line of seahorses
ride up towards the true mirror as we float
together in your large bath, steam rising
around us and I sink between your legs,
lean back against your breasts and smiling
you pour water over my face, my hair,
again and again as if I had just emerged,
needing to be woken up and well cleaned
before you could help me onto dry land.

ATTEMPTED BALLAD FOR THE MAN
TRAPPED ON THE LETTER C*

I hate whoever drew me like this,
with only a head and sneer,
my single eye staring out,
at my thirteen hundredth year.

And I hate this page of new beginning,
a word that becomes a God.
I hate the grin on John the Divine,
that drugged up silly sod.

And I hate the noise after closing time
when darkness falls around:
the crazy birds, the howling dogs,
the fucking cats abound.

For there is no peace within this book,
there can be no heaven here.
And there is no good news to be had,
just my life eternal, I fear.

*There are very few human figures in the Lindisfarne Gospels. One of the strangest is a head that appears within a decorated letter on the initial page of St. John.

AT THE END OF THE WALK

There should have been a photograph;
that last imbalance making us
clutch at each other in mid-stream,
bare feet useless on sun-green rocks,
you trying to laugh and then not,
your hands now almost at my neck,
my fingers closing on your waist,
caught between standing and falling
and below us the water's blur,
its quicks and calms, our faint shadows.

AN ARTIST WAS HERE

                              among the rocks,
working a sand patch, ridging with care
every firm slope and shear, the water poured
between ribs, to show freshly cut light.
And later, the artist returning
with a scatter of fragments: frond tips,
egg swollen and green; shells broken, whole;
a fern stem dropped from some great height,
among three stones now facing east.
They have been set, half-buried, smooth islands
for the sun to touch only each equinox,
anticlockwise, activating crystals.
And later still, worm letters wait
for a tide to make sense around fresh prints,
the arrow feet pointed out to sea,
where crouched under the horizon
the artist applies more colour,
treads water, takes a breath, then dives,
pushes waves into place, singing their purpose:
break, break, break, be beautiful.

ALTERNATIVE ENDINGS

he gets the girl or some other mammal
or the mysterious stranger in the first scene
turns out to be his father, which explains everything
or it's the iceberg's turn to sink this time
or they give up looking for the leg
or the six pairs of twins in tights are reunited,
recognised, loved; also there is a final couplet
or the sheep dog forgets his trapped master,
tries to find a better flock
or a small brown dot appears on her face,
expands, collapses and the film burns
or the baby is sung awake by the monster
or a naked surfer paddles into the sunset
or she says Ha and leaves quickly
or the cavalry dismount, grow their hair,
help around the teepees
or the alien decides to talk to the chimps instead
or clouds part, that stumpy celestial finger points,
a choir begins and all our sins are forgiven
or the wooden boy stays wooden,
or the sub-titles fall from the screen
or the last tree is carefully wrapped
or it is not in fact not a dream he is not dreaming
or the doctor runs out of heart stakes in the crypt
or there is accordion musique
and rain runs down a window pane
or the camera pulls back slowly: two people,
beach, the eastern coast, full outline of our island,
our continent, our mainly blue planet, stars, the rest.

ALDRED THE GLOSSATOR

wrote between the lines his full mouthed translation
in insular miniscule, cursive and quick
as if it were business or the law; thinking himself unworthy
and most miserable, seeking the help
of God and St Cuthbert for a steady hand and hard eye
as the snow fell and the snow fell
in Chester-le-Street that winter and the light moved on elsewhere.

a small poem about the book

two dead languages
between illuminations
good news forgotten

TWENTY (INCLUDING DOUBLE WORD SCORE)

After their dessert,
they play by candlelight,
stars and a moon he made earlier.

She is well painted,
his moustache freshly waxed.
They may not be young, but are hopeful.

There are half-smiles,
quarter glances, stray hands
almost touch on a glass. Then gently, but firmly

on the o of her ovules
he lays throb, leans close,
breathes: "It could have been broth."

TWELVE STOPS TO THE COAST*

We all begin in darkness
peering forward with the driver
from Monument to Manors,
then out into the great heights and sun
of Byker, where a schoolgirl
eyes her book and future.
Beyond Chillingham Road
(accurate, but awkward)
we slip around the back of everything,
where each factory forgets its purpose.
At Walkergate, nothing happens,
watched by a camera, as I watch
the cranes of Wallsend approach,
writing in unknown alphabets
their unfinished love letters.
A squall blurs Hadrian Road,
but I hear the woman singing
to her good child behind me,
as we slide over this green valley
to Howden and Percy Main,
where Jena and Pete have been
busy before me, leaving their hearts.
No-one gets off at Meadow Well
and North Shields is the far, far east
from where we curve north
past Tynemouth, its ironwork
surviving over ragwort and here is the sea,
large, and Cullercoats, my stop,
where the footbridge has been washed
clean of piss at last and Debussy
is always playing and now,
I am walking to your white door.

*These are all stations on the Tyne and Wear Metro, from Newcastle to
Cullercoats.*

37

THE RED GLOVE

beached on the middle shore, palm down
and sand filled; the finger tips cracked,
perished by the salt and the cold
and the labour, pulling and cutting
with its lost mirror twin and now waiting
for the tide, to start searching again.

THE ONE

My elder brother told me,
when they had all gone,
when we were alone in her house,
making the division:
you were always falling over,
you were the one she kept on picking up.

THE MAKING OF VELLUM

Little brother, pray and strike one true blow
to the forehead. String up the body,
ignore that twitching, cut the throat here,
let the blood fill this bucket and the next
and the next; slit the skin from arse to mouth,
pull out the guts, for the cook or the dogs.

Work quickly, little brother, so the hide
is still warm, ease it off the muscle
for the parchmenter to take and soak
in alum and lime; to stretch and scrape
and smooth and whiten, to cut to size
for our illumination, little brother.

Now imagine the pages licking
your hand as they turn, every word
wanting milk or a mother's touch.

THE ILLUSTRATED CALF

"The vellum pages of old manuscripts will take on the curves
of their original shape over time". *An Introduction to Book Restoration*
Knowles and Williamson

After various centuries the Book's pages
finally bent and realigned; escaped
their tight gatherings, the library,
and stood upright once more, four legged, wet nosed.

The covers sat in place on the animal's back,
like a saddle or stunted wings. Some words
became clearer: on its tongue caelorum,
along the tail beati qui lugunt. Fine initials

followed the lines of the ribs, in the fur
grew spirals and knots and between the eyes
a cross flamed. Of all the evangelists,
Mark came off worst, being far too close

to the arse for comfort. Now, Luke's healing hand
settles over the calf's heart and it shivers
in the rain, takes a second first breath,
kicks out, begins to gallop across the grass.

THE HOLE

that is a hole
it's six feet deep
people are standing around the hole
they look down into the hole
one man sees an arm
he asks is that my brother's arm ?
but in a foreign language
you will have to trust me that that is what he said
now the man says that is his ring, left hand, third finger, a gold ring
a woman says it could have been stolen; that could be his ring, but not his hand. I'm
looking for my mother
they all look into the hole
soil runs down into the hole

I made all this up, which may be a bad thing to have done
but I can see them looking into the hole
they all look into the hole
they all look down into the hole

THE DARKHOUSE KEEPER

Each night when the tide is low,
I work in my kelp garden,
rearranging the fronds for you,
shifting stones back into line.

Around me waves break themselves,
white fields grow by shoals and skerries,
islets are sharpened, worn down
and down and an hour before dawn

I return to the tower,
spiral up through the one wall
to the lantern room to cleanse
each prism and mirror and lens

and polish the one dark stone
at the centre. And I rest
until the first light, then set
the reflectors slowly turning,

gathering into themselves
a soft, black beam to pulse and shine
across the sea, towards the shore
and there pass over you without fear.

THE BEACH AT NEWTON

A small stream talks to the ocean,
having cut left and right through the dunes,
now broadening, losing depth, collecting the sun

and I stop where the flow meets the waves,
in dispute over well-ribbed sand,
as a gull settles, folds, unfolds;

then drifts off on the wind,
loaded with quiet, heading further north
where it is darker sooner; and this was not intended

to be here without you at the stream's mouth,
in December, listening to the lowering surf.

THAT PATCH OF SUNLIGHT WHICH

the red slug, my favourite of all gastropods
enters naked from the left shade, then pauses,
tentacles raised, taking the air, so nervous
of any first touch. Its eyespots are weak,
but know the difference between light
and dark
       and this red slug glows through
its full body tattoo, broken coils
and ridges flowing around the mantle
towards the single pore; a breath,
another and deeper still a memory
of shell settles
         as the red slug moves on,
over leaf skeletons and half-eaten seeds,
making more waves on its mucus bed,
frill undulating along the sole's edge.
It exits far right; now in light, now shade.

SPEAKING ABOUT MY CRACKED SUMP

I tell her about the pool
under my car each morning,
its blackness, the successive
seven drips I must always
count; watching what should be held,
released. She nods. Go on. Go
on. But only if you want
to. Her encouraging smile.
I say that the oil is like
a shadow resting there. I
say that one day it will spread
from beneath my car and flow
down this road. Babies and pets
will skate over it. There may
be confusions. Then the oil
will turn right at the junction,
and swamp the small roundabout,
mount a kerb, soak towards the
edge of our fine promenade,
stop by the railings, listening
to the waves below and drip,
troubling the water. She has
a question for me. Are you
the oil or the water ? I pause.
I am the skating baby
and I am the final drop.

SOME COLOURS OF THE BOOK

Those rocks and life forms,
all ground in a hard place for God;
then fixed in clarea and fish glue.
Here is cinnibar, limonite and malachite;
lamp black, chrome yellow and gold.
Here also is lapis lazuli, much travelled,
from the mines of Badakhshan,
now ultramarine for Mark's tunica.
Haematite is the blood stone,
ore and oxide; siricum the rust
on a pallia, also each dot.
Pour vinegar on fresh copper
to make verdigris and a lion's mane.
Add kermes to cerrusite for the flesh
of all faces. Someone must have walked
the Middle Ocean's edge collecting
oak galls and the intruder's eggs,
for Luke's plump, red cushion
and someone must have picked turnsole
and woad for their purple and blue;
(add wood ash, quick lime and stale urine
to your taste) and someone must have filled
the great white spaces with psimithium
and in each halo painted orpiment, arsenic rich.

PRACTISING OUR ART

For Ruby

I am figurative, but naive:
two adults, a child by the river.
You are primitive-abstract,
using both hands and a piece of toast.

"Very organic," your mother remarks,
"She's transforming her experience
of breakfast, making it other."
You smile at us knowingly,
throw back your blond hair, laugh,
being at this time well beyond language.

POEM IN HEAVY RAIN

Our tent breathing the wind
and the downpour pouring down;
each drop heard, only dots,
encoded, nonsense
from a much higher place

and I feel the pressure rising
all around us and I listen to the stream
cutting deeper and closer
and you sleep cry a message:
something important about love, about love.

PLAYING AT WAR AND LOVE

In the dark, much further up the valley,
there are Forces and Manoeuvres.
Some advance, others retreat;
all are blackened, dressed in moor grass
and fern, running with sweat from hole
to hole; have wide, white eyes.

This will go on for hours: the firing,
the flares drifting down, the night jets
cracking the air; but when the truce
is made, when it is finally all over
and quiet, I should call you.

PHOTOGRAPH

udcloudcloudcloudcloudcloudcloudcloudcloudcloudcloudcloud
cloudskyskyskyskycloudcloudcloudcloudcloudcloudcloudjetclo
udcloudcloudskydaymoonskycloudcloudcloudcloudcloudcloud
loudcloudcloudcloudcloudcloudcloudcloudcloudpossiblesunclo
dhelicopterclourainrainrainraincloudcloudcloudcloudcloudclou
cloudcloudcloudrainrainrainraindcloudcloudhillcloudcloudclou
illcloudcloudcloudrainrainrainrcloudcloudhillhillhillcloudcloill
hilldwoodwoodwoodwoodwoodwoodhillhillhillhillhillhillhillhil
illhllhillhillwoodwoodwoodwoodwoodhillhillhillhillhillhillhillh
woodwoodfieldfieldvillagevillagerivervillagevillagefieldtankfie
woodwoodfieldfieldfieldvillagevillagerivervillagefieldfieldfield
dwoodwoodvillagevillagevillagerivervillagefieldsmellbadsmells
odwoodvillagevillagesmokevillagerivervillagefieldholeholefield
dwoodwoodvillagevillagevillagevillagerivervillagevilfibadsmell
woodwooillagesmokevillagevillagesmokebodyvillagefieldfhole
menmenmendoodwovillagevillagevillagevillagerivervillagevfiel
menbodiesmenwoodwoovillagesmokevillagevillagerivervillagev
menbodiesmendwoodwoodlagevillagevillagesmokvillagerivevil
menmenmenoodwoodwoodillagevillagevillagevillagevillagerive
oodwoodwoodwoodwoodwillagevillagevillagevillagerivervillag

OUR SAINT'S DAY

and the church
is blessed
with holy water
and salt
as the tallows
spit into shadows
and the cantor
takes the Book
from the altar,
raises it high
and we follow
in faith and pairs
to the great west doors
and out into air
and sunset,
through silver puddles
to the high ground
with a view
above the lowest of tides
to face that line
on the horizon
that is Inner Farne
where the Saint's
last breath
still rests

and the cantor's arms
are shaking
with the weight
and the torches flare
with a breeze
that turns the pages
slowly: random
good words,
evangelists
and illuminations
spilling and shining
in the last
of the light
as the night birds
return and call,
unseen,
over fresh salt
and mud.

ON BECOMING SCRIBES OF THE LORD

Let the parchment
be your white conscience,
scrape it with the fear of God,
removing all sins; smooth it with heaven's desire,
whiten it with the chalk of holy thought.

You should rule all pages
with His will, write upon them
with the love of many neighbours
in ink of lamp black and humility.

Your desk shall be a tranquil heart,
rest upon it and copy from our Lord's life,
His heart; our redeeming exemplar.

If you gaze up from your labours
see only heaven

and blue sky.

NORTHERLY

Starved hedges just hold the fields in place,
plantations sit heavy on the fall and rise
to rough ground where the storm scatters gorse
and buildings among the first hills
and this sky without clouds is losing the sun,
but making planets, satellites, a moon;
identified objects, below which you drive home
through the light and half-light and less,
as my reflection grows in the window
and something wants stirring behind me
and again this house needs your weight.

UNDRESSING AT HOME

She's standing by her bed
taking off her blouse.

She pulls it over her head,
but hasn't undone

enough buttons
and is caught, starts to struggle,

which is when she remembers
what always came next.

appendix

ANDREW WATERHOUSE INTERVIEWS ANDREW WATERHOUSE ABOUT HIS COLLECTION *IN*

They are at a desk by a window in an upstairs room in November.

AW: I want to start with the title … plain, monosyllabic.

AW: Yes.

AW: It's also the title of a sequence of poems that deal with an illness and a recovery. Then there's the Van Morrison lyric you chose as the epigraph; about breathing in and breathing out. Poetry as therapy is a loaded subject, but I get the impression that you often use writing as a way of clearing out and externalising what is sometimes difficult. Is that right?

AW: Maybe.

AW: So what are your poems about then?

AW: A river, men travelling, the comet, apples, not, blond persons, a forest, Prothiaden, the end of the world, mica, grey, my belt and laces, knowing better, goats, the busy kingdom, half-smiles, Captain Picard, Kruger 60, Brother Moth, "Love", be pedalling, *The Sharpest Stone of the Mountain*, white ash and guilt, marzo, my mother, the last storm, infirm peat, soup, a brother's guitar, continence, the right crystal, memory of his birth, fish, hard places, the snake under the stone, cardigans, mucus, white, iron, the touch, mowing, red, still working, Ruby, two more leaves, a diving bandicoot, devotions, mid-step, grandfather, you, *San Miguel*, assumed restraint, something good and wholesome, the large ocean.

AW: I see. You often mix the real and fantastic in a single poem. Is that another escape strategy?

AW: Probably.

AW: Some history … you were born in 1958 in

Gainsborough, Lincolnshire; your parents ran a pub called the Cross Keys; you have a brother; you became a grammar school adolescent, worked on a farm for a year (stacked bales, harvested potatoes, fed cattle), went to university, taught, went to university again, taught again. You are currently resting. Are your poems basically autobiographical and self-obsessed? Are they "true"? Do you always tell the truth?

AW: Yes. No. No.

AW: The particular voice of your poems, I was interested in that: quiet, controlled, knowing, rational even in its excesses, understated, ironic. Metaphor seems pretty well absent.

AW: Could be me. And I can't do metaphor.

AW: As a compensation you play around with different registers: the under-languages of travel news, Chinese courtiers, tourist brochures, botanical texts.

AW: If you say so.

AW: I was thinking about The Characteristic Waterhouse Poem: a short lyric in free form, about fourteen lines, italics, footnotes, Significant Capital Letters, dialogue, fussy punctuation (especially; 's); mention of family, other species, crouching, home, a primary colour. Is that a fair summary?

AW: Yes

AW: Repetition, repetition; as well. You also like lists. Some cumulative effect gets slowly built up.

AW: I hope so. I make a lot of lists.

AW: The only traditional forms I could see are haiku and sonnets. Even the sonnets are loosely handled. Aren't you embarrassed about the haiku? Were they workshop exercises?

AW: There's something perfectly proportioned about the sonnet. It's a good length for me … I just run out of words in longer pieces. It's pliant, infinitely variable, can cope with mistreatment and survive. Also, I'll ignore your haikist tendencies.

AW: Some of your freer poems do have organising principles though, even if these are random or playful - all the lines in

Nightmare end in 't', the stanzas in *My Firewood Therapy* are continually bisected, the two views of the tree in *Rowan* mirror each other.

AW: Right. I need some constraint to work against. These fairly arbitrary limitations are actually liberating in a way.

AW: I've struggled to find much full rhyme in the collection, but you like half-rhyme. Is that because it allows unobtrusive patterning?

AW: Yes and it's far easier.

AW: You use varying line length in the poems, but set metres seem absent.

AW: Not my strong point. I've had long line periods and short line phases. I also struggled with line endings for a long time. They didn't seem to work; too abrupt or laboured or emphasising the wrong word, or something inconsequential.

AW: I'm interested in your writing practise.

AW: I have a biro and scruffy notebooks. I usually sit down, sometimes I stand or lie. Then there's the computer. Drafts. The usual.

AW: I've seen you in the library, downstairs in the reference section. A pile of books; last week you had six on gastropods, five on lighthouses, three on numerology. You scan read them, jot down words, smile. Is this Significant Research, being somewhere warm or just avoiding actual writing?

AW: All of those.

AW: What is the first poem you remember reading and being moved by?

AW: *Bavarian Gentians*. We did Lawrence for 'O' Level. All those *Last Poems*, read in December 1976. It was a very hormonal time.

AW: At home you have all of Elizabeth Bishop and James Wright, some Heaneys, a Smith (K) and a Didsbury, two McMillans, Herbert, all the Patersons. Those are the ones I remember. Is that a fair set of influences?

AW: Yes.

AW: Did you want to be Peter Reading once?

AW: Maybe, but now I'm feeling better (no disrespect meant, of course).

AW: What/who has helped your poetry?

AW: Workshops, Peter Sansom's *Writing Poetry*, my *Poet's Manual and Rhyming Dictionary*, Northern Arts, New Writing North, going to the Spanish Pyrennees, a month in Ireland, that blond person, Linda France, Jo Shapcott, David Stephenson, Earl Grey, decaffeinated Kenyan organic.

AW: I remember your first poem, published in 1984 (*Poetry Nottingham* Vol. 38, No. 2, p.28). Then there were others in *Stride*, *Tollgate Journal*, *Krax*. None of them got into the collection.

AW: You're embarrassing me. I was very youngish. It was a pre-apprenticeship. I'd like to apologise to the editors/reader.

AW: Then you gave up for five years, moved to Northumberland, began to actually read poetry a little, got published in other magazines, went to readings/more workshops, met a man in an Italian restaurant who brought out your first pamphlet, did an MA in Creative Writing, self-published another pamphlet, had a couple of joint exhibitions of poems/paintings with artist friends, pestered publishers to do a full collection, pestered publishers to do a full collection, pestered publishers to do a full collection, pestered publishers to do a full collection, pestered publishers to do a full collection, pestered publishers to do a full collection, pestered publishers to do a full collection, pestered publishers to do a full collection, and eventually got there. Did you enjoy putting the book together?

AW: I loved it. It seemed very, very important to get it as right as I could. I was desperate to make the book as coherent as possible. Spent days with ten year's worth of poems laid out in the spare bedroom. Made lists: definites, probables, possibles, the unreadables. A final selection. Sent them to Michael, got His Editorial Judgement and Suggestions. Then the ordering and shapefinding, tried: two parts, three parts, no parts, dark to light, light to dark, grey to grey, a peak in the middle, a peak at the end, a double peak, summitless, alphabetical by title, alphabetical by first line, favourite verbs together, favourite nouns together, chronological, circular, spiralling, emotional, by place, by time of day, random. Then someone said, "What about using *In* as the title poem, splitting it up and arranging all the other poems around the fragments?" So I did. All sorts of linkages appeared naturally. By chance the first poem's main character is the River Trent and the last word of the last poem is "ocean".

AW: Now, the difficult part. I've heard some criticisms of your writing: you try too hard to be clever, it's just chopped up prose; it's glib, loose, callous, evasive, underworked, thin, too resolved.

AW: Could be. I can only be aware of these and do my best.

AW: How would you like your poetry to develop in the future?

AW: I want to write poems longer than a page, try some new forms (sestinas seem wonderfully bizarre), engage with rhythm, do some dramatic monologues, be optimistic, attempt the occasional metaphor, get out more.

AW: We are getting close to the word limit. What are you doing now?

AW: Looking out of the window.

AW: And?

AW: It's a little dirty, the sun is angled and shining, there's leaves on grass, a full stream coiling, sheep, a mini-bus driving past.

AW: Do you want to ask me anything?

AW: No.

AW: Andrew Waterhouse, thank you for talking to me.

This interview first appeared in The Rialto, Issue Number 47 Winter 2000.

POETRY PUBLICATIONS BY ANDREW WATERHOUSE

Need-Fire (24 pp) The Bay Press 1996
In (68pp) The Rialto 2000
Good News from a Small Island (28pp) Mid Northumberland
Arts Group 2001
2nd: The Second Collection (64pp) The Rialto 2002

A Night at The Plague and Nausea (CD) Words by Andrew Waterhouse
Music by Stella Davies and others. Distributed by the Rialto.